DEALING WITH
**MENTAL
DISORDERS**

DEALING WITH
SELF—INJURY
DISORDER

By Tammy Gagne

ReferencePoint
Press®

San Diego, CA

LIBRARY OF CONGRESS CATALOGING-IN-PUBLICATION DATA

Names: Gagne, Tammy, author.
Title: Dealing with self-injury disorder / by Tammy Gagne.
Description: San Diego, CA : ReferencePoint Press, [2020] | Series: Dealing
    with mental disorders | Includes bibliographical references and index. |
    Audience: Grades 10-12
Identifiers: LCCN 2019034012 (print) | LCCN 2019034013 (ebook) | ISBN
    9781682827956 (hardcover) | ISBN 9781682827963 (ebook)
Subjects: LCSH: Self-injurious behavior. | Self-injurious
    behavior--Treatment. | Self-injurious behavior in adolescence.
Classification: LCC RC569.5.S48 G34 2020 (print) | LCC RC569.5.S48
    (ebook) | DDC 616.85/82--dc23
LC record available at https://lccn.loc.gov/2019034012
LC ebook record available at https://lccn.loc.gov/2019034013

CONTENTS

FEELING A SENSE OF DESPAIR

The weather had been sunny and warm all week, but Zoe felt anything but cheerful when she opened her text messages and saw the group invitation. Riley was having a pool party on Saturday. Everyone knew Riley was a bully, but no one wanted to become the target of her attacks. Riley took advantage of every opportunity to make fun of other girls, Zoe in particular.

Prom had been a prime example. A group of girls had planned to wear color-coordinated dresses to the event. Zoe's friend Gina had invited Zoe to join in. Riley had instructed all the girls to wear black, but each dress had to be different. Each girl agreed to share a selfie in her dress from the fitting room with the rest of the group.

Zoe had hated clothes shopping since she gained weight the previous year. Her antidepressant medication slowed her metabolism, causing her to go up two sizes. After trying more than a dozen dresses, Zoe reluctantly snapped a series of photos in front of the mirror. She chose the

People who self-injure may choose clothing that covers any scars they might have. This allows them to hide their disorder from friends and family.

only dress that covered all her scars. After applying two filters, she finally hit the send button.

Gina posted the first comment: *OMG! Love it! You look so pretty!* Gina had invited Zoe shopping the day before, but Zoe was scared her friend might see her scars. The smile that filled Zoe's face upon reading Gina's words faded as she saw Riley's response: *Had no idea such gr8 dresses came in plus sizes. JK, you look cute!!!*

Zoe cut herself again that night. She didn't go to the prom, but she saw pictures of the other girls posing at the event. Riley stood at the center in a white strapless dress with a black sash circling her tiny waist. Just thinking about it made Zoe feel sick.

Zoe wished that she had never started cutting herself. She hated the way her arms and legs looked now. She had promised herself that she would stop, but this behavior was the only thing that made her feel better. When her therapist had asked if she'd ever thought about hurting herself, Zoe lied. She had considered telling Gina, but she wasn't sure she could trust Gina not to tell the other girls at school. And she knew they would all be talking about her if her secret got out. It was easier to keep cutting and not tell anyone.

MANY PEOPLE HAVE SELF-INJURY DISORDER

The above story is fictional, but many people deal with overwhelming emotions by hurting themselves physically the same way that Zoe does. The behaviors go by several different names. Self-harm, self-mutilation, and self-wounding are a few of those names, but the clinical term for deliberately causing physical harm to oneself is non-suicidal self-injury (NSSI). A 2018 survey revealed that one in four girls in the United States took part in self-injuring behaviors. In some regions the numbers are even higher. Boys also use self-harm as a way of coping with bullying, stress, and negative emotions. Because so few people spoke about self-harm publicly in the past, it may seem like self-injury is a new trend. In an article she wrote for the *New York Times*, journalist Emily Baumgaertner stated, "The C.D.C. [Centers for Disease Control and Prevention] only recently began asking adolescents about self-injury, so it is unclear whether there has been a significant uptick in prevalence over generations."[1]

Actress Megan Fox is among the celebrities who have spoken openly about self-injury. Bringing up this topic can help increase education and awareness on the issue.

In recent years, however, some people have become more willing to share their struggles with self-injury disorder in hopes of raising awareness about this mental disorder. Megan Fox has a successful television and film career, but when she looks at herself she does not always see the glamorous actress that others see. In an interview with *Rolling Stone*, Fox shared that she had cut herself in the past due to feelings of low self-esteem. "I never think I'm worthy of anything," she admitted. "I have a sick feeling of being mocked all the time. I have a lot of self-loathing."[2]

> "I never think I'm worthy of anything. . . . I have a sick feeling of being mocked all the time. I have a lot of self-loathing."[2]
>
> – Actress Megan Fox

A survey published in the *Journal of the American Medical Association* suggests that self-harm is on the rise. Between 2009 and 2017, self-harm nearly tripled in girls between 10 and 14 years of age. Among 15- to 19-year-old girls and women, the problem increased 63 percent, and the behavior rose 22 percent in women between 20 and 24. During this time depression has also become a much more common mental health diagnosis. Are young people today simply willing to speak more candidly about their mental health problems than previous generations? In an article she authored for *Psychology Today*, psychologist Jean M. Twenge wrote, "That's unlikely, given the lengths to which the survey administrators go to ensure anonymity and the large, sudden increases in depression."[3]

Once a person begins self-injuring, it can be difficult to stop the behavior without professional help. In a 2017 article for *US News & World Report*, professional counselor Raychelle Cassada Lohmann explained, "Many teens who self-harm aren't trying to make their lives worse; they are trying to make it better. They don't like feeling the way they do, they just don't know how to make themselves feel better."[4]

Often, the most difficult step is the first one: sharing the secret with another person. A trusted family member or friend can help a person who is self-harming find a mental health professional who treats self-injury disorder. Sometimes people agree to get help after a friend initiates the conversation. Asking if a friend is self-injuring can be difficult and uncomfortable. But as CBS journalist Daniel Schorn wrote in a piece about self-injury, "[I]t's better to ask and be wrong than not ask at all."[5]

"Many teens who self-harm aren't trying to make their lives worse; they are trying to make it better. They don't like feeling the way they do, they just don't know how to make themselves feel better."[4]

– *Professional counselor Raychelle Cassada Lohmann*

CHAPTER **ONE**

WHAT IS SELF—INJURY DISORDER?

Anger, frustration, and sadness are just a few of the many emotions that can make people feel overwhelmed at times. Everyone experiences these and other negative feelings at least once in a while. Developing positive habits for coping with them—from listening to music or working out to writing in a journal or talking to another person—is ideal. For many people such activities provide a welcome relief from stress or other pent-up emotions, but others struggle with finding healthy coping mechanisms that work for them. Some of these people turn to destructive behaviors instead.

NSSI is a condition that compels people to harm themselves, making shallow, yet painful injuries to the surface of their body as a means of coping with anxiety or pain. The exact criteria for the condition are still under debate, but the proposed criteria require that five or more incidents occur over the course of a year. Although it is often referred to as "cutting" because of that common method of self-harm, self-injury can also include

Listening to music is a common strategy people use to cope with negative feelings. But some people instead feel compelled to resort to destructive behaviors.

a variety of other behaviors such as burning, scratching, hitting, rubbing, or biting oneself. It can even include a behavior called embedding, which involves inserting small objects such as unfolded paper clips underneath the skin. It does not include certain socially accepted behaviors that damage the skin, such as getting tattoos and body piercings.

The idea of self-injury may seem counterintuitive to those unfamiliar with this behavior. They may wonder why people in distress would want to add to their emotional pain with physical pain. Most people, after all, try to avoid pain of all kinds whenever possible. Psychiatrist Armando Favazza is the author of *Bodies Under Siege: Self-Mutilation, Non-Suicidal*

Self-Injury, and Body Modification in Culture and Psychiatry. As he explained during an interview on National Public Radio, "[T]he fact is that most self-mutilators do not feel pain when they mutilate." Instead, they feel a sense of relief from the emotional pain. They enter a mental state called dissociation which protects them from the physical feeling of self-harm. "What's being done is being done to their body," said Favazza, "but it's not being done to them because they're kind of floating out there away from their body."[6]

People with self-injury disorder feel an emotional relief when harming themselves, but the calmness is only temporary. It is quickly replaced with guilt or shame for their actions. Eventually, the underlying feelings that overwhelmed the person in the beginning return. The result is a cycle of self-harm that becomes increasingly difficult to stop without professional help.

Carrie Arnold is a science journalist who was diagnosed with self-injury disorder. In a piece she wrote in *Aeon* magazine, she described how her own self-harm led to more of the same. "The problem was that the embarrassment of cutting, the knowledge that these marks would become permanently tattooed into my skin, and the fears that someone would discover my secret, meant that any relief was short-lived. All too soon, I was feeling worse than before, leaving me

> "The problem was that the embarrassment of cutting, the knowledge that these marks would become permanently tattooed into my skin, and the fears that someone would discover my secret, meant that any relief was short-lived. All too soon, I was feeling worse than before, leaving me vulnerable to repeat episodes of psychic pain, followed by even more cutting."[7]
>
> – Science journalist Carrie Arnold

vulnerable to repeat episodes of psychic pain, followed by even more cutting."[7]

To better understand how someone with self-injury disorder feels relief from self-harm, it helps to know how the human brain processes pain. By studying this complex organ, scientists have learned more about the connection between physical and emotional pain. The brain senses emotional pain in a few different areas. One is called the anterior insula. This small part of the cerebral cortex is located behind each ear. Another area is called the anterior cingulate cortex. This piece of tissue is found toward the front of the brain. These are actually the same areas of the brain that sense physical pain. People with self-injury disorder stimulate their emotional pain receptors when they make themselves feel physical pain. As the physical pain peaks and begins to subside, they feel a release of emotional pain at the same time.

Many people develop self-injury disorder in their early teens. A number of situations can lead to self-harming behaviors, including bullying and other mental illnesses. Arms, legs, and torsos are the most common targets for the injuries, as they are areas of the body that are within easy reach and which can be easily covered. People usually perform these behaviors when they are alone, and they conceal the marks left behind by wearing long-sleeve shirts or long pants, even when the weather is warm. Parents, friends, and other loved ones often have no idea the self-injury is taking place at first.

One mother wrote an article for the *Telegraph* about her daughter's experience with self-injury disorder. The newspaper changed both their names to protect their privacy. Anna shared in the piece that she had been completely shocked to learn that her fifteen-year-old daughter,

Bullying is one factor that can contribute to self-harming behaviors. Studies have shown that those who are victims of frequent bullying are more likely to self-harm than others.

Sophie, had been injuring herself for about a year. "[Sophie's] adolescence had, like that of many girls, been a period of increasing turbulence—but self-harming never crossed my mind," Anna wrote.[8]

She discovered what Sophie was doing when her daughter called her one day asking if she could take a taxi home. Anna agreed after Sophie said she had cut her foot and that it hurt too much to walk to the subway. When she returned home, Anna quickly realized that her daughter needed medical attention right away. In addition to a fever, Sophie also had a purple mark rising up her leg. The doctors at the hospital diagnosed Sophie with cellulitis, a serious bacterial infection. She was admitted for a three-day course of intravenous antibiotics.

When Sophie changed into her hospital gown, Anna saw that her daughter's problem was far worse than she had realized. The girl had a ladder of scars on her arms, some obviously newer than others. What Sophie's parents had at first assumed to be an accident was actually a pattern of cutting behavior that would need to be evaluated by a psychiatrist.

HOW SELF-INJURY CAN BEGIN—AND ESCALATE

When people with self-injury disorder become upset, managing emotion often feels impossible without resorting to self-harm. For many people who self-injure, these emotions center around interpersonal difficulties. At first the self-injury may simply serve as a distraction from the emotional pain. They cannot control their mind, so they focus on self-harm because it is something they can control. The irony of this situation is that the more that people self-injure, the less control they have over the behavior. They need to do it even when the relief they feel from it lessens.

Some people with this disorder report feeling numb in situations where other people might feel pain, so they self-injure to feel something. Others feel the pain, but they do not know how to process it. They use self-harm as a way of communicating their emotions, even if no one else is present to witness the expression. They are simply trying to get it out. Still others may self-injure as a way to punish themselves. This driving force is common among people who have been victims of abuse. Although they have done nothing wrong, they worry that they are to blame.

Every situation is different. Some people perform self-injury a few times and stop on their own, but many others find that the behavior becomes a hard-to-break habit. Some mental health providers go as far as describing self-harm as addictive. They think the behavior stimulates a release of endorphins in the brain. These chemicals block pain and cause pleasure. They are also released when a person takes certain drugs, such as opioids. People with self-injury disorder do not know how to stop, or they feel they can't.

Clinical psychologist Ellen Hendriksen wrote an article for *Psychology Today* about self-injury. In the piece she addressed the addictive quality to cutting in particular. "Cutting can be notoriously difficult to stop on your own," she reported. "That harsh inner critic is a voice not easily silenced."[9]

As self-harm becomes more frequent, loved ones may notice the scars from the injuries. When first asked about the marks, many people with self-injury disorder may lie about their causes, fabricating stories about cooking mishaps, cat scratches, or other accidents to explain the wounds on their bodies. People who self-harm may also abstain from activities that involve baring one's arms and legs, such as swimming.

Thirteen-year-old Sydney Deneke's self-injury disorder began with one or two episodes of cutting a week. Soon, though, she was self-harming several times a day. Her mother, Pam, saw cuts on her daughter's hand while the two were riding in the car one day. Not knowing how to explain to her mother what she had been doing, Sydney lied. Her grandmother had just gotten a dog. The frightened teen claimed that the animal had scratched her.

Pam knew that the wounds she saw were not the result of interaction with the new pet. She gently asked her daughter if she was cutting. Sydney finally answered truthfully. It wasn't easy for Pam to initiate the topic of self-injury with her daughter. As a mother, she was frightened and

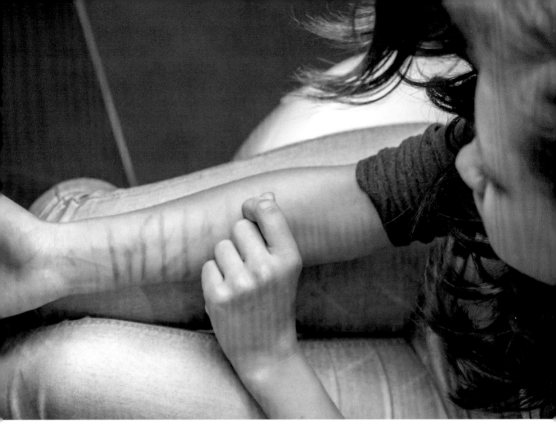

Self-harm scars may become apparent to friends and family over time. Recognizing such wounds is important in helping the person who is self-harming.

worried for her child's safety, but the conversation became the first step to getting Sydney the help she needed.

Many concerned loved ones mistake self-harm as an indication of suicidal feelings, because both can lead to injuring oneself, but as professional counselor Raychelle Cassada Lohmann explained in an article she wrote for *Psychology Today*, "The underlying mindset between someone who is suicidal and someone who self-harms is very different."[10] The difference is in their intent. A person who self-harms is actually trying to cope with life, not end it. Still, one cannot assume that suicide is not possible with someone who self-injures.

As the disorder progresses, the physical effects of self-harm can become increasingly serious. Although self-injury behavior is not a suicide attempt, the injuries that result from it can cause a person to die. Cuts made too close to major veins or arteries, as well as infections, can become life-threatening even without suicidal intent. Also, people who self-harm can develop suicidal feelings. Some studies have revealed that self-injury disorder is more common in people with family histories of suicide. Self-harm is a serious situation in any case.

TALKING ABOUT SELF-INJURY

Discussing self-harm can be difficult for both the people with the disorder and the people concerned about them. Those who self-injure know that others may find the topic disturbing—self-injuring people may even find it upsetting themselves. They may feel embarrassed or ashamed. Some people turn to self-injury because it is too difficult for them to communicate their feelings to others. A person with self-injury disorder may react negatively to being asked if they are self-harming. They may yell, cry, or outright refuse to have the conversation at all.

This does not mean that family or friends should avoid the topic if they suspect someone close to them is self-harming. Talking about self-injury disorder is often what helps get the person on the road to recovery. Although concerned individuals may hope that the problem goes away on its own, ignoring self-harm keeps the behavior a secret and can ensure that it continues or worsens. Still, it is easy to worry about saying the wrong thing or making the situation worse. The best way to begin a conversation is with concern and a willingness to help.

Laura Greenstein is a communications manager for the National Alliance on Mental Illness (NAMI). In a 2018 article on the NAMI website,

Talking about sensitive issues like self-injury can be challenging. Demonstrating compassion and concern for the person who is self-injuring is important.

she wrote, "The most important part of talking to someone about self-harm is to frame the conversation in a supportive and empathic way. Show concern for their well-being and be persistent if they don't open up right away."[11] Greenstein recommends avoiding judgment and body language that can be interpreted as critical, such as shocked or disgusted facial expressions. Although it may be tempting to try to lighten the mood, never joke about self-harm. Continue listening even when the details might make the conversation uncomfortable. Encourage the person to get professional help for stopping the behavior, and don't forget to follow up. One conversation may not be enough.

MENTAL HEALTH STIGMAS

Talking about self-injury can also be tough for loved ones. Part of the reason is the unfortunate stigma that can accompany mental illness. Loved ones may worry that their friend or family member will be judged by society if their self-harm becomes public knowledge. People may not want to be labeled by a mental health diagnosis. This is why some people who discuss their experiences publicly ask for anonymity when journalists share their stories about self-injury disorder. Sometimes others judge or discriminate against people with this and other mental issues, but by discussing problems such as self-harm openly, attitudes can evolve. People often fear what they don't understand. Education about self-injury disorder can lessen this fear—and by extension lessen the stigma surrounding mental disorders.

People with mental health concerns need treatment, just as people who suffer from physical illnesses do. Society does not judge a person with a heart condition for having a heart attack—or for needing medicine to lessen the risk of having another one. People who self-injure are likewise not to blame for their condition. Courtney Gavitt is a staff writer for the University of Connecticut's *Daily Campus* newspaper. In a 2019 article for the publication about self-injury disorder, Gavitt explained, "By helping decrease the stigma around [self-injury disorder] and making the subject less taboo, our society can have more open discussions that help connect people to the resources they need."[12]

Having conversations about self-harm can also be a way to prevent some people from developing self-injury behaviors. These people may begin by simply thinking about self-injuring, but education can lead them to resources that will teach them how to interrupt these thoughts before self-harm becomes a reality. There are many treatments for managing self-injury disorder. The same methods that people use to prevent recurrences of self-harm can be used to avoid the behavior in the first place. Seeking help from a mental health professional can also help identify any underlying causes for the desire to self-harm, such as

HOW SOCIAL MEDIA IS CHANGING TO HELP

With so many people spending large amounts of time on social media, some who self-harm have begun posting about their behaviors on these services. Some people have written about their desire to self-injure while others have posted photos of their scars. Some users have even gone as far as posting graphic videos of self-harm behaviors. Some social media platforms are working to create a way for users exhibiting signs of self-injury disorder to get the help they need without encouraging others to self-harm.

In 2019, both Facebook and Instagram announced that they would not allow any graphic images that promote self-harm. The sites would, however, allow users to post about their self-injury urges and past experiences—including photos of healed scars. Instagram's Adam Mosseri told a BBC reporter, "I might have an image of a scar, where I say, 'I'm 30 days clean,' and that's an important way for me to share my story. That kind of content can still live on the site."

Both sites have also created methods for concerned users to report posts that appear to be a cry for help. Facebook has even implemented an algorithm that identifies posts containing suicidal threats and alerts the user's local emergency services so first responders can check on the individual who may be in crisis.

Quoted in "Instagram Vows to Remove All Graphic Self-Harm Images from Site," BBC News, February 7, 2019. www.bbc.com.

Online resources can be either helpful or harmful. Searching for information from trusted authorities and experts can be a safe way to start.

anxiety and depression. Treating these problems may be enough to prevent the development of self-injury disorder altogether.

Online resources have both helped and hurt people with self-injury disorder. On the positive side of things, the internet has helped create conversations about a dangerous behavior that has long been kept a secret, bringing a spotlight to the problem. Raising awareness about the disorder is an important step in educating others about it. Many people also find it easier to discuss challenging topics online than in person. Conversely, the internet is not always the most credible information source. Moreover, not everyone who posts online has good intentions. Ill-intended individuals even use online forums to encourage other people to perform self-injuring behaviors. Clinical psychologist Carla Marie Manly notes, "Such forums might feel validating and supportive at the outset, yet they tend to perpetuate the highly destructive behaviors rather than address and heal them."[13]

Young people who are struggling with managing painful feelings are particularly vulnerable to peer pressure to self-harm. Many adolescents crave acceptance, and sometimes the place they find it is with other young people who have already begun this self-destructive behavior. Martin Gauthier is the psychiatrist-in-chief at the Montreal Children's Hospital. He explained in an interview with Erika Tucker of *Global News* that many kids get the idea to self-injure from the people around them. "Self-mutilation is very contagious. It is obvious on a psychiatric ward as it spreads from one patient to others. The same phenomenon exists obviously in schools and in our society through the examples given by stars, actors, musicians, and other teens."[14]

WHEN TO SEEK HELP

Many people who self-harm will attempt to downplay their self-injuring behavior after family or friends discover it. This can lead worried loved ones to hope that the problem will go away on its own. Jeannie Lerche Davis interviewed David Rosen, professor of pediatrics at the University of Michigan, for a piece about self-harm for WebMD. Rosen told Davis, "Kids who develop this behavior have fewer resources for dealing with stress, fewer coping mechanisms. As they develop better ways of coping, as they get better at self-monitoring, it's easier to eventually give up this behavior. But it's much more complicated than something they will outgrow."[15]

Even one instance of self-harm is enough to warrant seeking help for the behavior. Having a professional evaluation can prevent the problem from becoming a bigger one if the self-injury remains a secret. Starting a conversation about self-injury disorder may not convince people who are self-harming to stop right away, but it can make them realize that getting help is an option. It can encourage them to turn to the people they feel most comfortable talking to. Other family members or friends, family physicians, teachers or school counselors, and spiritual leaders are all excellent resources for this initial step.

If a self-injury becomes a medical emergency, the person will need to see a doctor as soon as possible. Concerned parties should call for an ambulance immediately in this situation, as it could quickly become a matter of life and death. Most hospitals will perform a mental health evaluation after a person is treated for an injury due to self-harm. They may also follow up by arranging outpatient services to help diagnose and manage the condition.

Sometimes the person who is self-injuring is the one to start the first conversation about it. Ann Matthew worried extensively about telling her best friend that she self-injured, but she thought it was important. In a blog post Matthew wrote for The Mighty, a digital health community that connects people facing health challenges, she confided, "As a human being, I feel the need to cover up the 'ugly' parts of me. But both the ugly and the pretty parts of us make us who we are." She added that despite her fears, she thought telling someone was a good thing. "I need to open up to someone I trust, just like many other people struggling with self-harm with no one to talk to yet."[16]

"I need to open up to someone I trust, just like many other people struggling with self-harm with no one to talk to yet."[16]

– Ann Matthew, on telling a friend about her self-injury

24

NONFATAL SELF-INJURIES
AMONG YOUTH,
2001–2015

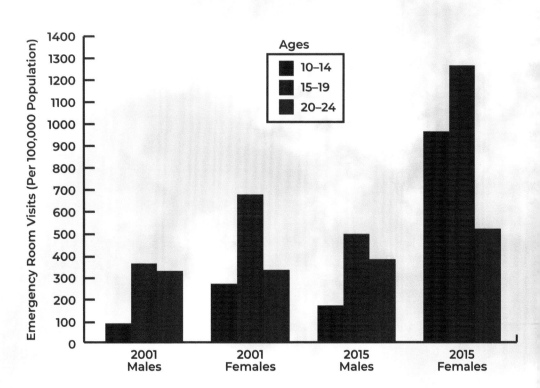

Emergency Room Visits (Per 100,000 Population)

Ages
- 10–14
- 15–19
- 20–24

| | 2001 Males | 2001 Females | 2015 Males | 2015 Females |

Melissa C. Mercado, Kristin Holland, Ruth W. Leemis, et al, "Trends in Emergency Department Visits for Nonfatal Self-inflicted Injuries Among Youth Aged 10 to 24 Years in the United States, 2001–2015," JAMA, November 21, 2017. www.jamanetwork.com.

CHAPTER
TWO

HOW IS
SELF—INJURY
DISORDER
RECOGNIZED?

With public discussion of self-injury becoming more prominent and open in recent years, it may be easy for people to assume that this psychological condition has only existed in modern culture. History reveals, however, that some people have actually been trying to relieve their emotional pain through self-harm since ancient times. In 490 BCE, the ancient Greek historian Herodotus wrote about a Spartan king named Cleomenes who cut his own shins with a knife.

For many centuries people dismissed behaviors that they did not understand by judging them as too dangerous to discuss openly. This is a common, but shortsighted, reaction to anything people fear, even in the modern era. Some people worried that by talking about dangerous behaviors such as self-harm, they could unintentionally prompt distraught individuals to perform those behaviors. The nineteenth century, though,

Some of the earliest study of self-injury was on a phenomenon revolving around sewing needles in the 1890s. However, self-injury continued to receive little public attention until many decades later.

marked the beginning of an increased interest in mental health. Doctors spent more time studying people with mental disorders, even those for which there was no name at the time. Self-injury disorder was among these mysterious afflictions. Staff members at mental hospitals and prisons observed that certain patients and prisoners were self-harming. Wanting to better understand the behaviors, doctors began observing these individuals more closely. Still, it would be many years before mental health professionals learned enough about this problem to diagnose or treat it.

In the 1890s, New York physicians George Gould and Walter Pyle documented an apparent fad that was becoming increasingly common in Europe. Large numbers of women were puncturing their skin with sewing needles. Some were even inserting the sharp metal objects underneath their skin and leaving them there. One woman inserted 217 needles into her body in a year and half's time. Sewing was a ubiquitous activity among women of the Victorian era, and it is likely that the women used needles because they were the most readily available instruments for self-injury. Still, the press focused on the tools as much as the behavior, nicknaming the young women "needle girls" when the disorder itself still had no name.

Gould and Pyle determined that the women who performed this odd behavior were suffering from hysteria, a catchall diagnosis of the era that male doctors often gave to women when they did not know exactly what was happening. Cornell University professor Joan Jacobs Brumberg, who specializes in social history and human development, explained, "The early writing on this was of the tone that this was just another lunatic hysterical female behavior."[17] While Gould and Pyle shined a light on self-harming behavior, they quickly swept it back under the carpet by labeling it before they fully understood it. Some people continued to self-injure, but few people outside the mental health community discussed it much.

> "The early writing on this was of the tone that this was just another lunatic hysterical female behavior."[17]
>
> – Cornell University professor Joan Jacobs Brumberg on self-harming behavior

THE MODERN ERA

Self-injury was brought back to public awareness about a century later when one of the most famous women in the world shared that she had intentionally injured herself. In 1995, Princess Diana of the United Kingdom told a reporter that she had cut her own arms and legs in the past because of emotional pain she was feeling. Diana's many fans struggled to understand why she would harm herself, but their concern for her well-being inspired many of them to keep an open mind as journalists began writing more stories to educate readers about self-harm. In the years that followed Diana's trailblazing interview, more researchers began devoting their time to the study of self-injury. The world was finally moving past shock over the existence of self-injuring behavior and toward compassion as well as a desire to understand it better.

Patricia and Peter Adler were among the first scientists to conduct extensive research about self-injury. The Adlers spent ten years interviewing 150 people from all over the world who shared their stories about self-harm. They also studied more than 30,000 internet posts in chatrooms dedicated to the behavior. The couple shared what they learned in their 2011 book *The Tender Cut: Inside the Hidden World of Self-Injury.*

As ethnographers—anthropologists who study individual cultures—the Adlers offered information that mental health professionals had yet to discover. They found that self-injury was afflicting more groups than just female adolescents. Other early studies focused mostly on affluent, white teenage girls who were being treated for self-injuring. "These studies are limited," wrote the Adlers, "because they used people in therapeutic or hospital settings as research subjects, who represent only the tip of the iceberg of the broader self-injuring population. When you look at the rest of the iceberg, at people in their 'natural settings' who self-injure, you will see a whole different demographic."[18] People who self-injure, the Adlers revealed, included male and female teens, adult men and women, people of different races, homeless people, people from different financial backgrounds, and even elderly people.

Today's mental health professionals are aware of self-injury issues and discuss them with patients. Including self-injury in the *DSM-5* means that professionals are using consistent information.

When mental health professionals attempt to diagnose a patient, they turn to the *Diagnostic and Statistical Manual of Mental Disorders (DSM)*. This publication of the American Psychiatric Association is a widely accepted guide for diagnosing mental illnesses. The text lists an astounding number of illnesses along with detailed descriptions, symptoms, and other relevant information needed for a reliable diagnosis. Like many other reference books, the *DSM* has gone through several incarnations over the decades. Each new version includes the latest information about new and previously recognized illnesses. The *DSM-5*, the latest version of the text, was published in 2013. It was the first edition to include self-injury, which it listed as non-suicidal self-injury (NSSI). The book included NSSI in a section covering "conditions requiring further study," calling attention to the fact that mental health experts are still learning about this disorder. It was not yet classed as a disorder that could receive a clinical, formal diagnosis.

Following its inclusion in the *DSM-5* as a condition for further study, self-injury disorder became an increasingly common topic among both mental health providers and laypeople. This behavior that people had been taking part in for centuries was finally being addressed as a condition worthy of further research. More people now regarded it as a problem for which people could seek treatment. More and more, they could also start talking about the behavior without as much judgment as self-injurers of the past had faced.

The good news was that the stigma surrounding mental illness was lessening with the attention the media was bringing to self-injury. Journalists were showing the public that most people who self-harmed weren't strange or morbid; they were simply overwhelmed by painful feelings and did not know how to cope with them. Unfortunately, stories about self-injury also provided some people who had not already been self-harming with the idea to start doing so. The Adlers discovered that some individuals who self-injured did so as a result of severe emotional trauma, while others turned to the behavior to cope with the more typical challenges of everyday life after learning that other people were doing it. It was especially common to see adolescents start self-injuring for these reasons.

The problem of self-harm being contagious remains an issue today. In a 2015 article for Canada's *Globe and Mail* newspaper, reporter Wency Leung wrote, "Those who deliberately hurt themselves tend to report having friends or online social networks who do it, too. Some researchers

WHO CAN DIAGNOSE SELF-INJURY DISORDER?

Only a licensed psychiatric professional, such as a psychiatrist or psychologist, can diagnose self-injury. Clinical social workers, counselors, and therapists are also trained to diagnose mental disorders, but when it comes to self-injury disorder, it is especially important to find a professional with experience dealing with this behavior in particular. Someone who specializes in self-injury is ideal. Since self-injury is commonly accompanied by other mental illnesses, it can also be helpful to seek diagnosis from a professional who treats the problems most commonly linked to self-harm.

Some schools provide a psychologist or counselor to their students. This can be a great contact for a person struggling with self-harm—or for a person concerned about a family member or friend who is self-injuring. Since some insurance companies require a referral for mental health treatment, a family physician can also be an excellent starting point. The insurance company itself may even be able to provide a person with a list of nearby health-care professionals.

People looking for a mental health-care provider should choose this person carefully. It is essential that the patient feels comfortable with the provider. The right match can make a big difference in a patient's long-term prognosis. Don't be afraid to ask questions. Among the most relevant concerns may be the specific treatment approaches and overall philosophy that a caregiver uses, as well as more basic information such as the provider's office hours and fees.

believe it can be socially contagious; hanging out with people who harm themselves may encourage some children to do the same."[19]

This may lead concerned family and friends to wonder how one tells the difference between a diagnosis for the disorder and so-called copycat behavior. Does the mere presence of self-injuring behavior mean that a person has the disorder? Not necessarily, but the behavior—particularly repeated incidents of it—is enough to justify an initial evaluation.

THE FIRST STEPS IN GETTING HELP

There are no universally agreed-upon criteria for self-injury disorder. Instead, a physician with experience dealing with the disorder begins by performing both a physical and mental exam on the patient. Since other mental health conditions often accompany self-injury disorder, tests for those illnesses may also be part of this process, especially if their symptoms are present. The diagnostic tools may include questionnaires or psychological tests. Sometimes the self-harming behavior is actually a symptom of another illness such as bipolar disorder, borderline personality disorder, or schizophrenia. The doctor's findings will help him or her choose the best treatment plan for the patient.

Some people see a doctor at the urging of family and friends who discover their self-harming behavior. Other people may have an unexpected conversation during a routine physical examination when their doctors notice scars or signs of more recent self-injury. Doctors are more likely to see the scars that a person usually covers with clothing because patients must undress for a full physical exam. Many people who self-harm become remarkably adept at keeping it a secret from those closest to them.

Actress and singer Demi Lovato began cutting herself when she was eleven years old. She quickly learned to hide the scars from her self-harming behavior from family and friends. "It started with my wrists," she told a writer from the British magazine *Fabulous*. "People saw that, so I cut in places they couldn't see."[20]

> "It started with my wrists. People saw that, so I cut in places they couldn't see."[20]
>
> – Actress and singer Demi Lovato

Lovato rose to fame as a child star on the Disney Channel. By this point in her life severe bullying had already driven her to bulimia, an eating disorder commonly associated with self-injury. Like many people who

HOW TO HELP A FRIEND WHO IS SELF-INJURING

Discovering that a friend is taking part in self-harm can be challenging. It can lead to a variety of intense emotions. At first, one may feel shocked or frightened. It is also common to feel angry or confused. A person might even resent the fact that the friend was keeping the behavior a secret. Furthermore, one might even feel obligated to keep that secret, especially if the friend asks that the information be kept private. A person who self-injures needs professional help, but there are things that a friend can do to help in this situation.

Offering to listen is good, and offering to go with the friend when she or he seeks help is even better. It is also good to tell a responsible adult, such as a parent or school counselor. The friend may get upset that their secret has been disclosed. The most important thing to do if this happens is remain kind and nonjudgmental. Getting angry or delivering ultimatums, no matter how well intended, could put more pressure on the friend to continue the behavior instead of getting help.

self-harm, Lovato was also depressed and eventually began using alcohol and recreational drugs to cope with her feelings. The eating disorder and addiction were part of her diagnosis. It is common for celebrities to feel enormous pressure to live up to unreasonable ideals. These people are constantly in the public eye, constantly subjected to the adoration—and criticism—of fickle audiences. When Lovato felt stressed by this pressure, she turned to unhealthy behaviors because they made her feel better in the short term.

A person who self-harms may promise to stop when loved ones express their concern. This had been the case for Lovato. Her mother, Dianna De La Garza, hoped that Lovato could simply stop her cutting, but she soon realized that it was too much for the teen to tackle alone. One morning when De La Garza went to wake her daughter in the morning, she found bloody rags next to her on the bed. She was relieved when she saw that the self-injury was not severe, and Lovato quickly promised not to do it again, but De La Garza still worried.

In 2018, De La Garza released a memoir called *Falling with Wings: A Mother's Story.* In it she wrote that she wanted to believe her daughter that day. "But the problem wasn't new," she acknowledged. "Demi had started cutting her wrists long before that morning. Once we noticed, we had a family meeting and decided to hire a life coach, figuring that if Demi could sort through the issues behind the cutting, she would stop. And she did. Everything seemed fine until I saw those bloody rags that morning."[21]

People who promise to stop self-injuring do not mean to break their promises. They just don't know how to do it without help. This is what makes diagnosis and treatment so important. Hilary Jacobs Hendel is a licensed clinical social worker who works with people with self-injury disorder. In an article she wrote for the NAMI, she explained, "Symptoms like self-harm won't go away until the individual has other ways to calm their emotional overwhelm. To ask someone to stop cutting without offering alternative ways to achieve comfort is akin to asking a trapeze artist to give up their safety net."[22]

> "Symptoms like self-harm won't go away until the individual has other ways to calm their emotional overwhelm. To ask someone to stop cutting without offering alternative ways to achieve comfort is akin to asking a trapeze artist to give up their safety net."[22]
>
> – Licensed clinical social worker Hilary Jacobs Hendel

Lovato finally decided to seek treatment in 2010 while on tour after her deteriorating mental state led to a physical altercation with one of her backup dancers. Her family staged an intervention following the incident. She decided to leave the tour and check herself into a rehabilitation hospital to seek the help she needed. Although Lovato has continued to struggle with her mental health in recent years, she says has gained much insight from the treatment she has received.

UNDERSTANDING RISKS AND TRIGGERS

People with certain mental illnesses may be more likely than others to self-harm. Those diagnosed with anxiety, depression, and eating disorders are part of this high-risk group. Likewise, the risk for self-injury disorder can also be increased by other circumstances. Young people who do not live with their parents, members of the LGBTQ community, and people who have lost loved ones to suicide also face a higher risk of self-harm. Each situation is different. Some people with high risk factors never self-injure—and some people not in high-risk groups do self-injure.

One might assume that if a person self-harms he or she automatically has self-injury disorder, but the process for recognizing this disorder can be complex, largely because there are so many reasons for and methods of self-harm. Many laypeople mistakenly think that self-injury disorder is limited to cutting, when in fact it can include a wide variety of behaviors. Although the exact method of harm can vary from one person to another, the common thread is the intent—to intentionally inflict physical pain on oneself.

In the moment of the act, the biggest goals of a person who self-injures may be to escape overwhelming feelings or resolve interpersonal difficulties. However, other motivators might also lead to the behavior. Some people who self-harm do so to make themselves feel something, to show others that they are in crisis, or to punish themselves out of self-hatred.

Abuse can lead people to feel bad about themselves. This, in turn, can be a cause of self-injury later in life.

Another group of people who frequently resort to self-injury are those who have experienced sexual abuse. Dr. Michael Hollander is the author of *Helping Teens Who Cut*. He notes in the book that teens who were sexually abused as children face a higher risk of not only self-harm but also suicide attempts. "One tragic consequence of early trauma," he writes, "is the child's belief that what happened was his or her fault. The legacy of this misguided belief is often intense contempt and self-loathing. For these children, self-injury can function as a self-soothing strategy and/or an expression of deep-rooted self-hatred."[23]

Even teens without abuse in their past or mental illness in their present can be vulnerable to self-injury disorder due to the extreme hormone changes that take place during adolescence. Natural fluctuations in hormone levels from puberty onward may make certain individuals more susceptible to mood disorders. This is particularly true for females. These changes, combined with the social challenges of the teen years, can lead a confused or overwhelmed adolescent to self-harm. In an article about self-injury, Janis Whitlock, a researcher at Cornell University, explained, "From a developmental perspective, you've got a perfect storm for self-injury."[24] The behavior can be especially common among teens with low self-esteem.

For a long time, scientists thought that girls and women faced the highest risk for self-injury disorder, but it now seems that this assumption was made because they are more likely to seek treatment. The most recent data suggests that self-harm behaviors are just as common in boys and men as in their female counterparts. Some of the same risk factors that lead young women to self-harm also make young men more vulnerable to it. They too experience problems such as low self-esteem, anxiety, and eating disorders.

Eating disorders were once almost exclusively seen in young women, but now problems with food and exercise are affecting young men as well. The media often projects an unrealistic body image for both sexes, and just like girls, boys feel pressure to try to live up to these physical standards. When their results fall short of what they see in magazines and on television, many young men feel like they aren't good enough.

When James Downs was a teenager in the United Kingdom, he didn't know how to handle difficult emotions surrounding his own body image. The only thing that seemed to help was dieting and exercising to the extreme. "I started to retreat more and more into my eating problems and self-harming behaviours as a way of avoiding having to cope with my feelings," he said in an interview with the *Guardian*. "It was to numb the emotional pain I felt with physical pain. Things got so bad that I lost my friends, had to leave school and gave up my university place. I felt like I was a failure and this only made my damaging behaviour worse."[25]

Until a diagnosis is made, it can be difficult, if not impossible, for many people who self-harm to stop the behavior. Just like alcohol or drugs, self-harm may feel good to the person doing it—at least initially. Soon, though, the behavior can spiral out of control, leaving the person feeling even worse than before they started hurting themselves. Self-injury disorder doesn't have to ruin a person's life, though. Seeking out a mental health professional to diagnose this illness can lead an individual to a treatment plan that helps end the behavior for good.

> "I started to retreat more and more into my eating problems and self-harming behaviours as a way of avoiding having to cope with my feelings. It was to numb the emotional pain I felt with physical pain. Things got so bad that I lost my friends, had to leave school and gave up my university place. I felt like I was a failure and this only made my damaging behaviour worse."[25]
>
> – *James Downs, who self-injured as a teenager*

CHAPTER **THREE**

WHAT IS LIFE LIKE WITH SELF—INJURY DISORDER?

Numerous individuals have come forward through the media in recent years to share their struggles with self-injury disorder with others who may be self-harming as well. Their stories can be found in newspapers, magazines, and online forums. Still, many people view the topic of self-injury as a bit of a taboo subject. Many parents are afraid to talk about the behavior with their kids, worried that they might unintentionally plant an idea in the head of an impressionable adolescent. Young people and adults who self-harm may also be scared of sharing their secret or of being judged for it. Unlike many other types of mental illness, which are often considered more approachable conversation topics, self-injury disorder remains a largely hidden issue.

Books, movies, and television shows frequently address dangerous behaviors such as substance abuse or mental illnesses such as

Amy Adams's portrayal of Camille Preaker in *Sharp Objects* put a spotlight on self-injury. Self-injury was a major part of the character's life as depicted on the show.

depression. Self-injury, however, is less commonly seen in the pages of novels or Hollywood scripts. People who self-harm often see themselves as oddities because they assume that others do not have this problem. They also do not see themselves represented in the books they read or the shows they watch.

Author Gillian Flynn created a prominent fictional character with self-injury disorder when she published her novel *Sharp Objects* in 2006. In 2018, HBO turned the book into a television series. Amy Adams plays the main character, Camille Preaker, a journalist who returns to her

Missouri hometown and her fractious family to cover a story. Preaker also self-harms. The show quickly drew its share of critics, but it also attracted viewers who were relieved to see their own mental health disorder depicted on television.

Among the latter group was freelance writer Samantha Mann. As a child, Mann frequently saw glimpses of herself in female book characters such as Harriet the Spy and Matilda. As she grew older, she identified with Kat Stratford from the film *10 Things I Hate About You*. Later, she looked to the women of Showtime's series *The L Word*, seeing parts of herself in them. Never, however, did Mann see a character struggle with self-injury like she did—until *Sharp Objects*. "Talking about adult self-harm seems like one of the last major mental health issues we haven't cracked open. I don't know why this seems to be the topic we've decided is 'too much,'" wrote Mann in a 2018 article for the women's magazine *Bust*.[26]

"Talking about adult self-harm seems like one of the last major mental health issues we haven't cracked open. I don't know why this seems to be the topic we've decided is 'too much.'"[26]

– Writer Samantha Mann

Living with self-injury disorder can be hard enough without feeling the isolation that comes with thinking that one is alone. In a piece she wrote for *TV Guide*, Kathryn Simpson revealed that *Sharp Objects* actually helped her confront her own problems with self-harm. Like many people who self-injure, Simpson kept her behavior a closely guarded secret. In the rare instances when she had seen her problem depicted on television in the past, she found it difficult to relate to the characters. "Characters who self-injure are often either so deeply dysfunctional, or so incredibly

RAISING AWARENESS WITH A CAMERA LENS

London photographer Jude Wacks created a project to raise awareness about self-injury disorder. The exhibit, called Best Days of Your Life, features a group of eighteen- to twenty-year-olds who self-injured when they went through difficult times in high school. The young men and women are dressed in simple black clothing for the portraits, which are meant to open a dialogue about the behavior. The mother of four teenage daughters, Wacks knows the pain and trauma that this disorder can cause families, as her daughter struggled with self-harm in the past. She also knows how prevalent the problem has become. In 2018 almost 1,600 people went to hospitals in London after harming themselves, yet self-injury is still is not talked about as much as other mental health issues. "I was very clear that I didn't want to glorify or glamorize in any way, but I did want to make people pay attention to it," she said during an interview with the BBC. At a showing of the exhibit in 2019, Wacks and her daughter led a discussion about self-injury and how it has affected their family.

Quoted in "Photographer Helps Young Talk Self-Harm," BBC, April 23, 2019.
www.bbc.com.

high functioning, that those of us who live between these binaries never see ourselves represented."[27]

Sharp Objects ended after its first season, but not because its ratings were poor. The show came to a close because its lead actress did not want to continue the show. Adams said that the role had led her to suffer from "nervous burnout." Playing certain characters can start to feel too real for some actors. HBO's president of programming, Casey Bloys, explained that Adams did not want to live in the character of Camille Preaker any longer. It seemed that even playing someone who self-injures can take a heavy toll on a person.

EFFECTS ON DAILY LIFE

Living with self-injury in the real world can be as overwhelming as the feelings that drive a person to self-harm. People who self-harm often feel irritable. They also feel guilt and shame for hurting themselves, as well as pressure to lie about their behavior. They may also seek out more private time so they can continue their self-harm without being discovered. Although they isolate themselves on purpose, this does not diminish the feelings of loneliness that come from spending so much time away from other people.

Loneliness and being ostracized are often the reasons that some young people seek out online self-injury forums to discuss their self-harm. Many people visit these sites so they can talk to others about their self-injury without feeling judged. Oftentimes, these forums are the only place people who self-harm feel comfortable being open and honest about the behavior. The benefit of reaching out to others in this way is that it may feel therapeutic at first, but the downside is that many people who visit these sites are not getting the professional help they need. The good that comes from reading and posting to these sites almost always gives way to continued overwhelming feelings, which can quickly propel the cycle of self-injury.

The cycle of self-harm makes many people feel trapped by the disorder. This is compounded by the fact that so few people discuss or truly understand this mental health problem. People who seek treatment can begin to understand the behavior better and learn effective ways to stop it, but even when people seek treatment, they often avoid telling others about this problem. Many people with more than one mental illness feel comfortable discussing other disorders with friends but find it difficult to bring their self-harm into the conversation. Dorothy Lane has been diagnosed with generalized anxiety disorder and panic disorder with agoraphobia along with her self-injury disorder, but she rarely talks about her self-harm. In an article she wrote for The Mighty, Lane revealed, "I think the reason I don't share my self-harm history is because the response I get most often is 'why?' and I don't have an answer."[28]

HOW SELF-INJURY DISORDER AFFECTS ONE'S RELATIONSHIPS

The most obvious impact of self-injury disorder comes in the form of the physical and emotional effects of the illness on the person with it, but this disorder can also have a significant effect on the person's family and friends. In the beginning, relationships may suffer when the person who self-harms pulls away, becoming more secretive and spending less time with others. Even if loved ones do not know what is happening, they may sense that there is a problem, especially if they had shared a more open and sociable relationship with the person in the past. Once they learn what is really happening, family and friends can experience a variety of feelings. The most common reactions to this news include shock, confusion, and fear.

David Prior is the executive director of Sunrise, a residential treatment center for teenage girls in Utah. In an article on the center's website, Prior addressed how self-injury disorder affects far more people than the person doing the self-injuring: "The individual who is doing the self-harming creates a reality in their own mind that they are only harming themselves. This is simply not true. Ask any family member of a self-harmer and you'll find that the effect on them is significant."[29]

Self-harm can affect those around the person who is hurting himself or herself. Disagreements over what to do about a self-injuring child can increase tensions in the parents' marriage.

People closest to someone who self-injures often spend a lot of time worrying about the person. Knowing that the behavior is different from behaviors with suicidal intent may be somewhat comforting, but loved ones might still worry about what could happen if the person unintentionally takes self-harm to a life-threatening level. Siblings may become frightened that the person who is self-harming might inflict harm on them as well. Although it is rare for a person who self-harms to hurt others, the fear can feel very real to those experiencing it, especially when they are younger kids.

Parents may feel like they need to walk on proverbial eggshells around a child with self-injury disorder. Sometimes one or both parents become too permissive, afraid that setting limits or saying no will trigger more self-harm. Mothers and fathers may also disagree about how to handle the situation, with one parent being more direct and the other reacting more passively. This can lead to conflicts in the marriage and added tension in the household. Some parents may handle their worry by becoming overly protective, feeling the need to keep potentially dangerous objects such as razors or knives locked away when they can't supervise their use. The desire to protect the child and prevent self-harming behavior can even reach the point of paranoia.

Some people may be so afraid of saying or doing the wrong things that they begin to withdraw from their relationship with the person who self-injures. Although they are not trying to worsen the problem, this response can intensify the loneliness the person who self-injures feels. Feeling connected to others is important for learning how to handle the overwhelming feelings that can lead to self-harm.

Much like the person who is self-harming, family members often feel compelled to keep self-injury disorder a secret from other people. They may feel embarrassed, worried that others will judge them. They might feel that telling their own friends about what is happening would betray the person who self-injures. This too can be isolating. Having friends to discuss the situation with can be helpful, especially if the friends have experience dealing with this or another mental disorder. Compassionate friends can be part of a vital support system for everyone.

EFFECTS ON SCHOOL AND WORK LIFE

Dealing with self-injury disorder—or any mental disorder—can make it difficult to focus on schoolwork and earn good grades. It can also lead to social isolation at school and elsewhere. To make matters even more challenging, poor performance in the academic setting has been linked to an increased risk for self-harm, making the pressures of school yet another part of the self-injury cycle. Young people who have earned good grades in the past may worry about disappointing their parents or themselves. This pressure can also trigger an urge to self-harm in some individuals.

Many teachers, other school faculty members, and school counselors are caring individuals who want to help their students succeed both in and out of a classroom. Sometimes a teacher may be the first person to notice the signs of self-injury behavior, alerting a school counselor or the student's parents. Unfortunately, not all educators respond to self-harm in a constructive way. Some may view self-harm as an attempt to manipulate situations or avoid the responsibility of completing schoolwork. These individuals may also dismiss self-injury as an attention-seeking behavior.

Framing the behavior this way implies that the student is simply looking to be the center of attention for fun. Kayla Chang knows about this situation. She began self-injuring when she was a child. Now an adult, she writes for a blog about self-injury. As she explained in a blog entry, sometimes people who self-harm are indeed seeking attention, but not in the way that some individuals assume. In this situation the self-harm is a cry for help. "What the self-harm is saying," wrote Kayla, "is, 'Something is wrong, and I need help, but I don't know how to ask for it.' This attention-seeking self-harm should be understood for what it is: not as a childish expression of inflated ego, but as a beacon signal for sympathy, safety, and support."[30]

Young people with self-injury disorder may worry about what will happen when they transition from the academic setting to the workforce. Will their bosses or coworkers judge them if they see their scars? If so, could this judgment hold them back from succeeding in the workplace? They may wonder whether they should tell someone—such as a human resources manager—about their mental health struggles or if it would be more prudent to keep these personal details a secret.

It can be difficult to focus on one's job duties while simultaneously worrying about becoming the object of gossip or being denied advancement for reasons unrelated to job performance. For some people these stressors can worsen self-injury disorder, triggering the cycle of self-harm. This can be especially dangerous if one's workplace includes tools or other equipment that people can use to self-injure, but even seemingly innocuous settings such as offices contain objects such as scissors and staplers. For those who are still grappling with the urge to self-harm, temptations lurk nearly anywhere.

Despite the possibility that some people will react adversely, it may be better to be upfront about self-injury disorder. In a 2019 article she wrote for *Glamour*, freelance journalist Caitlin Flynn wrote, "The reality is that some bosses will always be jerks, but most experts agree it's worth looping in your boss or HR department if your mental health is impacting

> "What the self-harm is saying is, 'Something is wrong, and I need help, but I don't know how to ask for it.' This attention-seeking self-harm should be understood for what it is: not as a childish expression of inflated ego, but as a beacon signal for sympathy, safety, and support."[30]
>
> *– Self-injury blogger Kayla Chang*

your job performance. Every employee should be safe to disclose her mental illness to her employer without fear of retribution—that's the law."[31]

LIVING WITH THE LONG-TERM EFFECTS

Living with the physical scars of self-injury can feel like wearing a sign that announces the disorder to the world. The scars can also serve as a reminder of painful times many people would prefer to forget. Looking at the marks can prompt emotions that remain challenging for people to process even as they move beyond the self-harm. They may feel shame, regret, or even confusion over how they came to perform these acts.

Colton Wooten is a freelance writer who self-injured as an adolescent. At first he hid the scars from the cuts he made on his arms and legs with razor blades and kitchen knives, but soon he stopped trying to keep these acts a secret. At this time self-harm took the place of the words he could not find to express his emotional pain. Years later, as someone who now makes his living with words, he feels like a different person. In a piece he wrote for the *New York Times* in 2018, he shared that it is now difficult for him to understand who he was when he hurt his body.

Although the physical scars remain, Wooten knows that he was fortunate that his self-injuries did not leave behind permanent damage. At one point he cut beyond the tendons in his left wrist, effectively disconnecting the communication between his hand and his forearm.

He had emergency surgery to save his mobility after this incident. "I knew that I had gone too far," Wooten wrote. "The surgeons acted fast and were able to repair my sundered tendons with tiny stents. They intervened early enough to rescue my nerves from atrophy, though I couldn't feel my thumb for a year."[32]

Many people with self-injury disorder have trouble creating and maintaining a positive self-image. Although some people might think of poor self-esteem as merely a confidence problem, it can actually go deep enough to cause a person to dislike or even hate oneself. A person who is self-confident trusts himself or herself to succeed in the world. But self-esteem has to do with how people feel about themselves. A person with high self-confidence may have low self-esteem. "This is also a feeling you cannot escape since you are always in your own company," freelance writer Sam Woolfe explained in a 2018 article for HealthyPlace. "At least if you hate another person, you can avoid him."[33]

As people who self-injure learn healthy ways to deal with their feelings, overindulging in certain coping mechanisms can become a new challenge. Some people find that the endorphins released through exercise help ease stress and other taxing emotions. Others find comfort in eating favorite foods, going to the movies, or shopping. In moderation these can be acceptable ways of treating oneself, but when done too often, they can become destructive patterns. Too much exercise or overeating can be symptoms of eating disorders, and spending too much money can place a person in debt.

One of the most common feelings that people who self-harm feel is a sense of otherness. Because the behavior is often met with so much disgust or confusion, people who self-injure may see themselves as

Running can be a great way to cope with negative feelings. Still, it is important not to overdo exercise or other coping strategies.

freakish. This can be especially difficult for young people. Sociologist Martin A. Monto, who has conducted extensive research on self-injury disorder, explained in a 2018 interview with the *New York Times* that parents, too, can suffer from this worry. "Parents who deal with this often think their child is a clinical anomaly. It's certainly not a healthy behavior—it's harmful," he acknowledged. "But if your child has done this, the data shows that it doesn't make them an unusually ill person."[34]

Seeking treatment is essential for lessening the risks for long-term physical and emotional effects of self-injury disorder. The urge to repeat self-harm can be strong. Often the only successful way to stop is by undergoing psychotherapy and learning new ways of managing overwhelming emotions. In the best scenarios, people get this help before they hurt themselves in irreversible ways.

More often, people who have self-injury disorder end up living with some lasting consequences of their self-harm. The list of these effects is long and varied. For instance, cuts heal, but the scars from them often become permanent. In severe cases of self-harm, people can lose limbs or suffer from serious infections or blood poisoning. The latter can cause secondary problems such as sleep issues, hallucinations, or panic attacks. Substance abuse, which can result from or accompany self-injury disorder, can become an addiction that people must deal with for the rest of their lives.

As lonely as people with self-injury disorder often feel, they may be surprised to learn just how many other people have gone through the same thing. This was the case for Vicki Duffy, who needed skin graft surgery because of the cigarette burns she inflicted on her arms. After she got help for her own self-injury, she went on to run a support group in New Jersey for people with the disorder, but she remembers well what it was like to walk around with the evidence of self-harm. One day a stranger who appeared to be in her seventies approached Duffy after noticing the burn marks. "I used to do that," the woman confided.[35]

CHAPTER
FOUR

HOW IS SELF—INJURY DISORDER TREATED?

Treating self-injury disorder is a highly individualized process. Each person who self-harms has a unique set of circumstances that led to the self-injury. Therefore, each treatment plan should address those circumstances. For example, a mental health professional treating someone who suffers from another mental illness will often begin by treating that condition in addition to the self-injury disorder. Psychotherapy, medication, and other therapeutic methods can all be part of this process. In severe cases hospitalization may be necessary.

A person with self-injury disorder must be patient after seeking help. The desire to self-harm will not go away overnight, no matter which combination of treatments a doctor uses. Successful treatment depends greatly on both the patient's desire to recover and a willingness to work hard for that recovery. Making lifestyle changes and learning new coping mechanisms, which also take time, will be necessary.

The first step in treatment may be for a person to talk to a general practice doctor about his or her concerns. The doctor can then refer the patient to a mental health specialist.

When talking to mental health caregivers, it is important to be up-front and honest. The only way a caregiver can help is by having thorough and accurate information. It can be useful to take a family member or friend along to the first appointment. He or she can stay in the waiting room during the actual evaluation, but simply having a loved one close by for support can be reassuring for many people. Some people prefer to have this person present for the evaluation as well, as loved ones can often help them recall details about everything from medical history to recent incidents of self-harm. Ideally, all adult members of the household should ultimately participate in the treatment process to minimize unhealthy responses to self-injury disorder. Communication among family members is essential to this process.

HOSPITALIZATION—A TOOL THAT'S SOMETIMES NECESSARY

Sometimes the fear of being hospitalized is what keeps a person from sharing the secret of self-injury. Not everyone who self-injures needs to be hospitalized, but in rare cases of life-threatening self-harm, a stay at a mental health facility can help keep people safe until they can learn how to manage the dangerous behavior. If a person is worried about being hospitalized, he or she should tell the mental health-care provider that this is the case. Confronting this fear by discussing it honestly may very well reveal to the provider that a hospital stay isn't required. If a person is clearly not suicidal and understands the forms of self-harm that constitute a life-threatening situation, outpatient therapy is often the preferred method of treatment.

HOW PSYCHOTHERAPY CAN HELP

Psychotherapy is the most widespread approach for treating self-injury disorder. One of the most common types is cognitive behavioral therapy (CBT), which helps a person who self-harms recognize negative thought patterns before they lead to self-injury. This approach also involves learning new coping skills, which ideally replace the self-harming behavior. Dialectical behavior therapy, a type of CBT, teaches people with self-injury disorder how to manage emotions so overwhelming feelings do not drive them to self-harm. Instead, they learn to better tolerate distress. This form of CBT also teaches people how to improve their relationships with others.

Psychodynamic therapy can help a person explore past experiences to better understand how they relate to self-harm. This approach can be useful for people who don't know exactly why they self-injure. Many times people who find it difficult to talk about their feelings can have unconscious motivations for both the behavior of self-harming and the emotions behind it. For instance, someone who self-harms as a way to cope with trauma from childhood abuse might not even realize that this is the reason for their self-harm.

Kim Johancen-Walt is a psychologist with more than twenty years of experience treating people with self-injury disorder. In an interview with *Counseling Today*, she spoke about treating a memorable patient by the name of Jennifer, who had self-injury disorder. This fifteen-year-old girl had an alcoholic mother and an absent father, a situation which contributed to Jennifer seeing herself as both invisible and undeserving. The teen said that she cut herself to "feel something."

Johancen-Walt shared, "I wanted to give her a corrective experience in our therapy that communicated that she was both seen and valued. I accepted her unconditionally and told her she deserved love and kindness throughout treatment. Although the old messages of self-hatred were still there, she now had a different way of defining herself. With my help, along with [that of] many others, she was eventually able to do what I now refer to as 'putting a wedge in the choke hold of self-injury.'"[36]

Johancen-Walt asked Jennifer to use alternatives to self-harm, such as placing a rubber band around her wrist and snapping it or placing an ice cube in her hand until it melted.

> "I accepted her unconditionally and told her she deserved love and kindness throughout treatment. Although the old messages of self-hatred were still there, she now had a different way of defining herself."[36]
>
> – *Psychologist Kim Johancen-Walt*

She agreed to substitute these behaviors in place of cutting herself when the urge to self-injure struck. During their therapy sessions, Jennifer even came up with alternatives of her own, such as going to a public place where it was socially unacceptable to hurt herself. She would stay there until the desire passed.

OTHER APPROACHES

The specifics of the therapeutic approach differ based on each patient's situation, but a mental health caregiver may ask a person who has been self-injuring to sign a contract agreeing to tell someone when the urge to self-harm occurs. The clinician may also ask a patient to keep a log of their behavior to help identify the times they are most compelled to self-injure and how they respond. Another approach involves an agreement that the person will postpone the self-injury by a certain amount of time—say, ten or twenty minutes, with the hope being that it will be enough time for the person to interrupt the behavior with another, healthier action. Journaling is another common approach, which can help patients get in touch with their feelings or explore the past.

Mindfulness therapy is often the key to preventing self-injury. Identifying one's triggers for self-harm is the first step in interrupting the behavior. Being able to employ practical distractions such as calling a friend, going to a movie, or going for a walk can sometimes be enough to stop the self-harm from occurring. It is also helpful to use self-care techniques as a proactive approach. Regularly taking part in activities such as listening to music, cooking, or reading can help a person manage emotions before they become overwhelming. Activities that relieve stress, such as yoga or dancing, can be especially effective.

Adena Bank Lees is a licensed clinical social worker who treats self-injury disorder. She uses an approach called experiential learning to help patients stop the cycle of self-harm. As she explained in a 2019 article for *Psychology Today*, experiential learning allows a person to learn

Journaling gives people the chance to organize and record their feelings. This may help them reflect and think about themselves in a new light.

by doing. She begins by acting out a scenario that might trigger self-injury for the patient. As they go through this step together, they discuss what is happening in detail. She then moves the conversation toward identifying healthy alternatives the person may use instead of self-harm. The patient then tries to use one or more of these techniques to handle overwhelming feelings the next time they arise. "If the individual does not feel comfortable or I assess she/he is not able to tolerate the level of affect necessary to directly act in the scene work, I have them watch someone else doing it," Lees wrote. "Learning by proxy can be just as powerful."[37]

Sometimes the key to managing one's feelings is learning to release them in a harmless way. When anger is among the overwhelming feelings, some experts recommend releasing these strong feelings by popping balloons or bubble wrap, ripping up or scribbling on paper, or going for a run. Sadness, too, can be expressed in healthy ways, such as watching a tear-jerking movie, listening to some sad music, or—if possible—speaking to a friend. The more energy that gets placed in expressing feelings in these types of ways, the less tempted a person may be to self-harm.

HELPFUL APPS

Although spending too much time on smartphones has been blamed for having a negative impact on mental health, certain apps for these digital devices could actually help people prone to self-harm. Initial studies show that certain factors such as typing speed, word choice, and even how often a person stays home could signal an increased risk of self-harm in certain individuals. These are just a few things that could detect—and ideally prevent—self-injury. Dr. Thomas Insel is a psychiatrist who thinks that smartphones could actually become a useful tool in managing mental illnesses. He claims there might be as many as 1,000 smartphone "biomarkers" for depression. Engineers are currently developing apps that could help identify times when a person is most likely to self-harm. The smartphone user would have to provide consent for such an app, but if successful, it could help turn a trigger for self-harm into part of the solution. Patients should let their health-care team know when they are using such apps.

Making connections with other people can be especially helpful for reducing feelings of loneliness. Calling family members or friends when overwhelming feelings appear can be a tremendous help, but it is also important to maintain these relationships at other times. Making plans with someone whose company is enjoyable gives a person something to look forward to. Some people also find great solace in the company of pets. Sometimes talking to a dog or cat feels less intimidating than sharing one's feelings with another person.

THE ROLE OF MEDICATION

Medication is most useful for treating the underlying conditions that often contribute to self-injury disorder. In these cases the medication often has a positive effect on self-harm. For example, antidepressants often help reduce the urge to self-injure when a person also has depression or bipolar disorder, since these medications improve the symptoms of those and other mental illnesses.

Only medical doctors can prescribe medication, so when a person with self-injury disorder takes an antidepressant to treat a condition related to self-injury disorder, it is typically prescribed by a family physician or a psychiatrist. Psychologists and other mental health professionals utilize psychotherapy for treating self-injury disorder but cannot prescribe medication themselves. However, these caregivers can work in conjunction with medical doctors for a collaborative approach if that is deemed best for the patient.

Caution should be used when beginning any new medication, but this is especially true for young people with self-injury disorder who start taking antidepressants. A study published in 2014 showed that starting teens and young adults on high doses of antidepressants can actually increase their risk for self-harm. It is important for people to take medications as prescribed, keep family members aware of their feelings, and let doctors know of any changes in mood.

Finding an effective medication and its ideal dosage is essential to the therapeutic benefit, but this can take some time. As clinical psychologist Deni Carise explained in an interview with the website Healthline, "Some antidepressants work better for certain people and different ones for other people. So if you get the right one, and bring up those blood levels very quickly, you do want to watch the person much more carefully."[38] For this reason it is important that a patient report any changes in behavior, including increased urge for self-harm, to a health-care provider after starting a new medication.

> "Some antidepressants work better for certain people and different ones for other people. So if you get the right one, and bring up those blood levels very quickly, you do want to watch the person much more carefully."[38]
>
> – *Clinical psychologist Deni Carise*

PROGNOSIS FOR SELF-INJURY DISORDER

Although the goal of treatment is to stop self-injury altogether, it can take time for the person to discontinue the behavior completely. In the most challenging situations, replacing the sensation of self-harm with another, more positive action can help. For example, some people find that taking a cold shower, clapping their hands loudly, or stomping their feet strongly provides a similar release as self-injury—but without the lingering effects. Some mental health experts recommend using a red felt-tip pen to draw on the skin instead of cutting it.

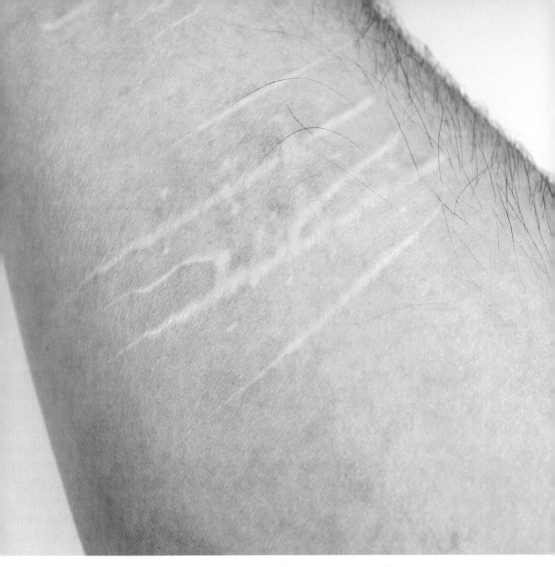

The scars of self-injury heal over time. Many people are able to recover from this mental health issue and stop self-harm for good.

In the most severe cases of self-injury disorder, progress is more important than the less realistic goal of discontinuing the behavior completely. In these cases success is defined by reducing the incidents of self-harm. People who self-injure may slip up and return to the behavior, but this does not mean that they cannot get it under control again. Negative behaviors can be hard to change. It is important for those who have this condition to be patient and continue to work with a health-care provider as they heal.

Many people with self-injury disorder have been able to stop their self-harm for good. A 2015 study revealed that three factors were the most common among these patients. Nearly 40 percent of them reported that they were able to stop cutting after they found that overwhelming feelings—as bad as they can feel in the moment—are temporary. These people became more capable of denying the urge to self-harm because they knew it would eventually pass. Another 24 percent credited loving relationships in their lives with helping them stop self-injuring behaviors. The nature of the relationships varied from romantic to familial, but each person reported feeling loved and valued by someone, which made it easier to stop the self-harm.

The third, and perhaps most surprising, reason which 27 percent of people shared for stopping the behavior was time. This group insisted that they simply outgrew self-injuring. Although this data may feel reassuring to people with the disorder and those who care about them, mental health professionals caution that time does not stop the behavior by itself. It appears that maturity does, however, make it easier for many people to succeed at discontinuing self-injury by using the methods that mental health providers give them.

Mary Hamilton self-injured for a decade before she was finally able to stop the behavior. "I am one of the lucky ones," she wrote in an article for the *Guardian*. "Not only did I survive—I recovered. With time, incredibly hard work, and help from more people than it's possible to count, I found better ways of coping with depression. Once it was possible, I managed to put down the razor blades and got on with life. It was depression that almost killed me. Self-injury kept me alive for long enough to work out how to stop it."[39]

When Olivia James stopped self-injuring, she shared her reasons through a piece she wrote for The Mighty. She pointed out that over time the release she once felt from self-harm became increasingly difficult for her to achieve from the behavior. "From my experience," she wrote, "after a while, you need to more and more to get the same effects. And eventually, it stops working completely. No matter how long you endure it, it won't make things right."[40]

Learning to stop one's self-harm can be especially challenging for people who do it as a way of controlling something in their lives. Lauren Coe was one of these people. Today, Coe is a crisis counselor in New York City, but for a long time she too battled self-injury disorder. In an article she wrote for *Psychology Today*, Coe explained that her self-harm began when she realized that there were so many things in her life that she couldn't control— from other people's actions to her own feelings. To her, self-injury felt like regaining some of that control. "I have been trying to get better at being okay with not having control. Always being in control means too much power and it's unrealistic. It can actually be a relief to let go of control and just let yourself feel whatever you need to feel. You'll get through it," she wrote, "I promise."[41]

> "I have been trying to get better at being okay with not having control. Always being in control means too much power and it's unrealistic. It can actually be a relief to let go of control and just let yourself feel whatever you need to feel. You'll get through it, I promise."[41]
>
> – Crisis counselor Lauren Coe

INCREASING THE ODDS FOR SUCCESS

People with self-injury disorder can increase their chance for successful treatment by taking an active role in their recovery. This begins with taking care of one's health—eating a nutritious diet, exercising regularly, and getting enough sleep, for instance. Maintaining a routine and following one's treatment plan can also help a person with self-injury disorder. It is especially important to take any prescribed medications on the recommended schedule.

When self-harm does occur, take care of the wounds adequately and promptly. This may mean making a trip to the emergency room for stitches or other medical treatment if the injury is severe. Never share items such as cutting instruments with others who self-harm, as this practice can spread blood-borne diseases. Preferably, reach out to someone before the self-harm takes place. Make a standing arrangement to call a specific family member or friend—or a mental health professional—if the urge to self-injure arises.

Avoiding alcohol and recreational drugs is another way people with self-injury disorder can stack the odds in their favor. Many people turn to these substances in an attempt to numb overwhelming feelings, but this temporary relief can come at a high cost. Alcohol and drugs can intensify feelings of anxiety and depression. It is easier to stick to a treatment plan and abstain from self-harm when a person also abstains from these substances.

LIFE BEYOND SELF-INJURY DISORDER

Shirley Manson, lead singer of the rock band Garbage, used to self-harm to manage her own overwhelming feelings as a young person. Although she thought she had put the behavior behind her, it re-emerged when

Having a supportive network of friends is important. It can help a person successfully recover from self-injury disorder.

Garbage rose to fame and she began feeling the pressures of the spotlight. In an article Manson wrote for the *New York Times*, she shared that she hadn't felt so self-conscious of her body since puberty. When numerous fashion magazines featured her photos on their covers, she couldn't stop comparing herself to others with an overly critical eye. The mental anguish she felt made her think about cutting herself again, but she worked hard to resist these urges. Although she still has overwhelming feelings sometimes, Manson wrote, "I vow to hold my ground. I choose to speak up. I attempt to be kind, not only to myself but also to other people. I surround myself with those who treat me well. I strive to be creative and determine to do things that make me happy."[42]

Going through a particularly stressful or otherwise difficult experience can trigger the urge to return to self-harm for many people who once found it helpful. Support groups can be useful to these individuals. In an article for the website HealthyPlace, Natasha Tracy shared, "It's important to develop a network of self-harm supports in an effort to get better. These are the people and places you can go to in the event that you're feeling a strong urge to self-harm."[43] Mental health organizations can direct people to in-person support groups. There are also some reputable online support groups.

Relapses are common with self-injury disorder, but that doesn't mean that a person cannot stop self-harm for good. Instead of focusing on the setback, people who return to self-injuring must look forward and renew their commitment to ending the behavior. Something many people find helpful is remembering how they initially stopped their self-harm. On the website The Mix, Anthony Burt wrote, "These strategies have already worked for you and may work again. You have found particular distraction techniques useful so you could try them again or try different ones."[44]

> "These strategies have already worked for you and may work again. You have found particular distraction techniques useful so you could try them again or try different ones."[44]
>
> – Writer Anthony Burt

How successful a person is at stopping self-injuring behaviors depends on many factors, but, as with any situation where change is desired, the most pivotal may be the person's level of motivation. Without a strong desire to get better, a person who self-harms is unlikely to stop. In a 2016 article for *Time*, a teenage girl named Phoebe shared her opinion that it is not possible to stop another person from self-injuring. "I tried making pacts with friends," she said. "But it doesn't work. You have to figure it out for yourself. You have to make the choice."[45]

SOURCE NOTES

INTRODUCTION: FEELING A SENSE OF DESPAIR

1. Emily Baumgaertner, "How Many Teenage Girls Deliberately Harm Themselves? Nearly 1 in 4, Survey Finds," *New York Times*, July 2, 2018. www.nytimes.com.

2. Quoted in Erik Hedegaard, "Megan Fox Draws Blood," *Rolling Stone*, October 1, 2009. www.rollingstone.com.

3. Jean M. Twenge, "5 Reasons Why Self-Harm and Depression Have Tripled in Girls," *Psychology Today*, November 21, 2017. www.psychologytoday.com.

4. Raychelle Cassada Lohmann, "Bleeding Away the Pain: The Ins and Outs of Self-Harm," *U.S. News & World Report*, July 18, 2017. https://health.usnews.com.

5. Daniel Schorn, "Teen Shares Self-Injury Secret," *CBS News*, June 6, 2006. www.cbsnews.com.

CHAPTER 1: WHAT IS SELF-INJURY DISORDER?

6. Quoted in Alix Spiegel, "The History and Mentality of Self-Mutilation," *NPR*, June 10, 2005. www.npr.org

7. Quoted in Colin Schultz, "There's a Scientific Reason Why Self-Harm Makes Some People Feel Better," *Smithsonian*, October 16, 2014. www.smithsonianmag.com.

8. Anna Stone, "Self-Harm: Why Would She Cut Herself?" *Telegraph*, October 2, 2013. www.telegraph.co.uk.

9. Ellen Hendriksen, "Self-Injury: 4 Reasons People Cut and What to Do," *Psychology Today*, October 20, 2016. www.psychologytoday.com.

10. Lohmann, "Understanding Suicide and Self-Harm," *Psychology Today*, October 28, 2012. www.psychologytoday.com.

11. Laura Greenstein, "How to Respond to Self-Harm," *National Alliance on Mental Illness (NAMI)*, March 1, 2018. www.nami.org.

12. Courtney Gavitt, "Self-Injury Awareness Day: Understanding Self-Harm and Ending the Stigma," *Daily Campus*, March 1, 2019. http://dailycampus.com.

13. Dr. Carla Manly. Personal interview. August 19, 2019.

14. Quoted in Erika Tucker, "Teen Self-Injury on the Rise, Becoming a Trend: Montreal Doctor," *Global News*, September 14, 2012. https://globalnews.ca.

15. Quoted in Jeannie Lerche Davis, "Cutting and Self-Harm: Warning Signs and Treatment," *WebMD*, n.d. www.webmd.com.

16. Ann Matthew, "Why I'm Scared to Tell Someone About My Self-Harm," *The Mighty*, October 10, 2017. https://themighty.com.

CHAPTER 2: HOW IS SELF-INJURY DISORDER RECOGNIZED?

17. Quoted in Jessica Bennett, "Why She Cuts: One Woman's Battle with Self-Injury," *Newsweek*, December 28, 2008. www.newsweek.com.

18. Patricia and Peter Adler, "Self-Injury: A Silent Epidemic," *CNN*, August 23, 2011. http://thechart.blogs.cnn.com.

19. Wency Leung, "The Cluster Effect: Is Self-Harming Contagious?" *Globe and Mail*, May 24, 2015.

20. Quoted in "Demi Lovato Admits to Depression and Self Harm in New Interview," *Psychological Care & Healing Center*, May 1, 2012. www.pchtreatment.com.

21. Quoted in David Canfield, "Demi Lovato's Mom Relives Darkest Family Moment in New Memoir: Read an Excerpt," *Entertainment Weekly*, March 5, 2018. https://ew.com.

22. Hilary Jacobs Hendel, "Why Some People Harm Themselves," *NAMI*, March 14, 2018. www.nami.org.

23. Michael Hollander, *Helping Teens Who Cut*. New York: The Guilford Press, 2017. p. 71.

24. Quoted in Rachael Rettner, "Why Do Teens Hurt Themselves? The Science of Self-Injury," *LiveScience*, September 12, 2010. www.livescience.com.

25. Quoted in Sarah Marsh, "A Quarter of Young Men Self-Harm to Cope with Depression, Says Survey," *Guardian*, March 1, 2017. www.theguardian.com.

CHAPTER 3: WHAT IS LIFE LIKE WITH SELF-INJURY DISORDER?

26. Samantha Mann, "Why *Sharp Objects* Portrayal of Adult Self-Harming Is So Important," *Bust*, August 20, 2018. https://bust.com.

27. Kathryn Simpson, "On *Sharp Objects* and Feeling Ruined," *TV Guide*, September 19, 2018. www.tvguide.com.

28. Dorothy Lane, "Why I'm Finally Sharing My Self-Harm Narrative," *The Mighty*, February 2, 2017. https://themighty.com.

29. David Prior, "The Effects of Self-Harm on the Family," *Sunrise*, February 29, 2016. www.sunrisertc.com.

30. Kayla Chang, "When Self-Harm Is for Attention," *HealthyPlace*, February 28, 2018. www.healthyplace.com.

31. Caitlin Flynn, "How to Talk to Your Boss About Your Mental Health," *Glamour*, March 27, 2019. www.glamour.com.

32. Colton Wooten, "Surviving Myself," *New York Times*, August 7, 2018. www.nytimes.com.

SOURCE NOTES CONTINUED

33. Sam Woolfe, "The Low Self-Esteem and Self-Harm Connection," *HealthyPlace*, April 11, 2018. www.healthyplace.com.

34. Baumgaertner, "How Many Teenage Girls Deliberately Harm Themselves?"

35. Quoted in "Self-Mutilation Rampant at 2 Ivy League Schools," *NBC News*, June 5, 2006. www.nbcnews.com.

CHAPTER 4: HOW IS SELF-INJURY DISORDER TREATED?

36. Quoted in Lynne Shallcross, "When the Hurt Is Aimed Inward," *Counseling Today*, June 1, 2013. https://ct.counseling.org.

37. Adena Bank Less, "Providing a Whole-Brain Approach to Treating Self-Harm," *Psychology Today*, March 6, 2019. www.psychologytoday.com.

38. Quoted in Shawn Radcliffe, "High Doses of Antidepressants May Rise the Risk of Self-Harm for Kids and Young Adults," *Healthline*, April 28, 2014. www.healthline.com.

39. Mary Hamilton, "How I Managed to Stop Self-Injuring and Get On With My Life," *Guardian*, March 1, 2012. www.theguardian.com.

40. Olivia James, "8 Brutally Honest Reasons I've Stopped Self-Harming," *The Mighty*, November 5, 2015. https://themighty.com.

41. Lauren Coe, "15 Things to Do Instead of Self-Harming," *Psychology Today*, August 7, 2017. www.psychologytoday.com.

42. Shirley Manson, "The First Time I Cut Myself," *New York Times,* July 3, 2018. www.nytimes.com.

43. Natasha Tracy, "Self-Injury Help, Self-Mutilation Help and Support," *HealthyPlace*, August 26, 2016. www.healthyplace.com.

44. Anthony Burt, "Having a Self-Harm Relapse," *The Mix*, September 29, 2015. www.themix.org.uk.

45. Susanna Schrobsdorff, "Teen Depression and Anxiety: Why the Kids Are Not Alright," *Time*, October 27, 2016. http://time.com.

FOR FURTHER RESEARCH

BOOKS

Sarah Chaney, *Psyche on the Skin: A History of Self-Harm*. London: Reaktion Books, 2017.

Michael Hollander, *Helping Teens Who Cut*. New York: The Guilford Press, 2017.

Erin Pack-Jordan, *Everything You Need to Know About Suicide and Self-Harm*. New York: Rosen YA, 2019.

Janice Yuwiler, *What Is Self-Injury Disorder?* San Diego, CA: ReferencePoint Press, 2016.

INTERNET SOURCES

"146 Things To Do Besides Self-Harm," *Adolescent Self-Injury Foundation*, n.d. www.adolescentselfinjuryfoundation.com.

Alia Dastagir, "The Cutting Storyline in '13 Reasons Why' Is Scary but True," *USA Today*, May 2, 2017. www.usatoday.com.

Alex Hopley, "Not All Self-Harm Looks Like Self-Harm," *The Mix*, March 1, 2019. www.themix.org.uk.

"How to Help in an Emotional Crisis," *American Psychological Association*, n.d. www.apa.org.

Amy Marsh, "The Girl Who Is Fighting Back Against the Addiction of Self-Injury," *Harness*, October 5, 2017. www.harnessmagazine.com.

WEBSITES

Crisis Text Line
www.crisistextline.org/selfharm

The Crisis Text Line is a free resource that offers real-time counseling over text messaging for those in distress, helping them become cooler and calmer.

S.A.F.E. Alternatives
www.selfinjury.com

This website offers resources and information about seeking help for self-injury disorder.

To Write Love on Her Arms
www.TWLOHA.com

To Write Love on Her Arms is a nonprofit organization that aims to find help for those suffering from depression, addiction, and self-injury.

INDEX

INDEX
CONTINUED

IMAGE CREDITS

ABOUT
THE AUTHOR

Tammy Gagne has written dozens of books for both adults and children. Her recent titles include *Online Shaming and Bullying* and *Women in the Workplace*. She lives in northern New England with her husband, son, and a menagerie of pets.